Devotion, Inspiration & God's Word

By:

Dee Evans

Copyright © 2020 Donavia (Dee) Evans

All rights reserved. No part of this publication may be reproduced, stored in a retrieval system, or transmitted in any form or by any means-for example, electronic, photocopy, recording-without the prior written permission of the publisher. The only exceptions are brief quotations in printed reviews.

Scripture taken from The Holy Bible, Old and New Testaments in the King James Version. Copyright 1976 by Thomas Nelson INC. Used by permission. All rights reserved.

For information about custom editions, special sales, premium and bulk purchases, please contact:
www.rise2write.com

Rise2Write Publishing LLC

DEDICATION

This book is dedicated to my son Mykah, and Children of the Most High God.

DEE EVANS

INTRODUCTION

My Holy Spirit led me to write this devotional book. I was in the process of writing my first urban fiction book, "Lies, Façade & Deceit: Life After a Toxic Marriage." My Spirit weighed heavily on me to stop writing that book and focus on this devotional. I tried to ignore my Spirit because I wanted to finish my first urban book.

At that time, I was not considering writing a devotional book; completing my first urban book was my priority.

Long story short, I listened to my Spirit and wrote this book in 22 hours, publishing it within 24 hours in eBook format. This is the first book I have ever published. Every word in this book is from the Most High God! Always remember, "When we tell the Most High God our plans, he laughs."

I pray this book is a blessing for you and serves as a spiritual reference guide.

PEACE & BLESSINGS!!

GOD'S IMAGE

Genesis 1:26

An God said, Let us make man in our image, after our likeness: and let them have dominion over the fish of the sea, and over the fowl of the air, and over the cattle, and over all the earth, and over every creeping thing that creepeth upon the earth.

Genesis 1:27

So God created man in his own image, in the image of God created he him; male and female created he them.

Genesis 2:22

And the rib, which the Lord God had taken from man, made he a woman, and brought her unto man.

Genesis 2:23

And Adam said, This is now a bone of my bones, and flesh of my flesh: she shall be called Woman, because she was taken out of Man.

Wisdom of Solomon 2:23

For God created man to be immortal, and made him to be an image of his own eternity.

❖

While enduring this Spiritual journey its good to always reference back to Creation. We served a purpose from the beginning of time. The book of Genesis shows us that we were created in God's image and likeness. It is especially important that we are reminded of this and that we understand that we are the creation of God in Heaven. God created each one of us with a purpose. Never feel as if you are living in vain and serve no purpose! Not only did God create us with a purpose but he Granted us the Dominion over all the Earth.

In the book of Wisdom of Solomon it shows that God intentions with man was for immortality which reflects God's own eternity. God created us to be an image of his Own Eternity which means his goal for his Children is eternal life. SMILE! We are Destined for Eternal Life through Jesus Christ!

****

Prayer:
Oh Father God in Heaven,
We thank you for this day and creation of men and women. We are so grateful for your love for us to create us in your

likeness and allow us to have dominion over all of Earth. We ask that you help guide us to not abuse this power and to serve your purpose with this power. In Jesus Name I pray!
Amen!

Devotion, Inspiration & the God's Word

GOD'S GRACE

Psalm 103:8

The Lord is merciful and gracious, slow to anger, and plenteous in mercy.

Titus 2:11-12

For the grace of God that bringeth salvation hath appeared to all men, Teaching us that, denying ungodliness and worldly lusts, we should live soberly, righteously, and godly, in this present world;

Romans 3:23-24

For all have sinned, and come short of the glory of God; Being justified freely by his grace through the redemption that is in Christ Jesus:

God's grace is Everlasting to those who seek him. How bless are we to have a Father who shows us unmerited favor even when we do not deserve it. Even when we fall short of his word, he never leaves our side. He is still there in the midst to pick us up. He sent his only son down from Heaven to die for our sins.

****

Prayer:
Oh Father God in Heaven,
We thank you for your Everlasting Grace and Mercy. For we know Lord that without your grace we wouldn't be where we are today. We ask that you continue to help deliver us from things of this world and guide our spirits to focus only on you and your word. We love you and cant stop praising you! In Jesus Name I pray!
Amen!

Devotion, Inspiration & the God's Word

DEE EVANS

GOD'S LOVE
1 John 4:16

And we have known and believed the love that God hath to us. God is love; and he that dwelleth in God, and God in him.

John 3:16
For God so loved the world, that he gave his only begotten Son, that whosoever believeth in him should not perish, but have everlasting life.

1 John 4:19
We love him. Because he first loved us.

Romans 8:35
Who shall separate us from the love of Christ? Shall tribulation, or distress, or persecution, or famine, or nakedness, or peril, or sword?

John 14:15
If ye love me, keep my commandments.

God's love for us is conditional based upon repentance and keeping his commandments/laws. Even though his love is conditional, God love cannot supersede! He loves us so much that he sent his only begotten son, Jesus Christ to earth just to give us another chance to get it right and die for our sins. He seen where we were falling short and he was still fighting and rooting for us to turn from evil. His arms are always open wide for us, while he is fighting on a daily for our attention and love. All we must do is lean on him and turn from evil, he will always be waiting for his children with welcoming arms.

We show our love for him through keeping his commandments. God is willing and ready to forgive us for our sins at any moment. No sin is greater than the other. All we must do is repent, keep the commandments, and turn back from sin.

****

Prayer:
Oh Father God in Heaven,
I thank you for your unconditional love!
Even during the times I don't deserve it

you are still by my side loving me, protecting me and guiding me. I cry out to you for forgiveness. For I am a sinner that wants to be cleansed from my sins. I am ready to turn from my sins and serve you Lord! Thank you for loving me unconditionally Lord! I ask for forgiveness and I will forever serve you. In Jesus Name I pray!
Amen!

GOD'S WILL

Jeremiah 29:11

For I know the thoughts that I think toward you, saith the Lord, thoughts of peace, and not of evil, to give you an expected end.
Psalm 143:10
Teach me to do thy will; for thou are my God: they spirit is good; lead me into the land of uprightness.
1 John 2:17
And the world passeth away, and the lust therof: but he that doeth the will of God abideth for ever.

God knew us when we were inside our Mother's womb. He works all things out according to your purpose. Everything that you are experiencing is aligning up for your will and nothing happens without the approval from God.

He will never allow more on you than you can bare or carry. It is all under control if you continue to believe and trust his will over your life. Our thought are not God's thought and we will never be able to

discern God thoughts. Continue to trust his will and surrender over to his will for he will not lead you astray.

****

Prayer:
Oh Father God in Heaven,
Even when it seems like you are not near me I trust that you are. I surrender over my own thoughts and ideas over to your will and understanding. I ask that you continue to strengthen my trust in you. I love you Lord and I know that you want the best for me. I just ask you to continue to build me up through your will and way.
In Jesus Name I pray!
Amen!

WALKING by FAITH

WALKING BY FAITH

2 Corinthians 5:7

For we walk by faith, not by sight:

Proverbs 3:5-6

Trust in the Lord with all thine heart; and lean not unto thine own understanding; In all thy ways acknowledge him and he shall direct thy paths.

Romans 10:17

So then faith cometh by hearing, and hearing by the word of God.

Hebrews 11:1

Now faith is the substance of things hoped for, the evidence of things not seen.

Hebrews 11:6

But without faith it is impossible to please him: for he that cometh to God must believe that he is, and that he is a rewarder of them that diligently seek him.

Walking by faith is hearing the word of God with no evidence by sight but believing wholeheartedly in the teachings from the Prophets of the Bible. We were never blessed to see the teachings of Jesus or the Disciples. This is where faith comes

in and is so important.

Our wisdom and knowledge come directly from the Bible teachings, keeping God's laws and commandments.

Even when the vision is blurry, and nothing seems to make sense or go accordingly. We must continue to stand firm in faith, trust God's word and not lean unto our own understanding.

Walking by faith is strengthens our relationship with God daily because we are trusting and believing in his word without ever seeing him physically but knowing he is present within us.

****

Prayer:
Oh Father God in Heaven,
I ask for forgiveness for all the times I drifted away from your path and leaned onto my own understanding. I trust in your word and teachings oh Lord. I ask for you to continue to strengthen and build my faith, wisdom and knowledge. I ask that you continue to stay near me and continue to direct my path. I love you and will continue to praise and honor your name. In Jesus Name I pray!

Amen!

ENDURANCE

Devotion, Inspiration & the God's Word

ENDURANCE

1 Corinthians 10:13

There hath no temptation taken you but such as is common to man: but God is faithful, who will not suffer you to be tempted above that ye are able; but will with the temptation also make a way to escape, that ye may be able to bear it.

James 5:11

Behold, we count them happy which endure. Ye have heard of the patience of Job, and have seen the end of the Lord; that the Lord is pitiful, and of tender mercy.

Romans 12:12

Rejoicing in hope, patient in tribulation; continuing instant in prayer.

Endurance is measuring your persistence. How persistent are you with praying, reading your Bible, keeping God's laws and commandments?

Do not loose focus or get off track! God is watching and the Angels are taking notes! Even when you feel like you are doing everything right and nothing good is happening... Continue to Endure! We

are tested daily because this is not our home. We are visitors on this proving ground. Whenever you feel like giving up and start to loose patience always remember and reflect on the book of Job!

Enduring to the end to reap eternal life is the final goal for us True Believers.

****

Prayer:
Oh Father God in Heaven,
I ask that you continue to give me the strength to continue to endure during times I want to give up. I pray for the spirit of Job to overcome me with patience, and faith. I pray for spiritual eyes to continue to fight this battle. For I will continue to rejoice through trials and tribulations because I know this is not my home and I am just a visitor. I trust in your will and your way. In Jesus Name I pray!
Amen!

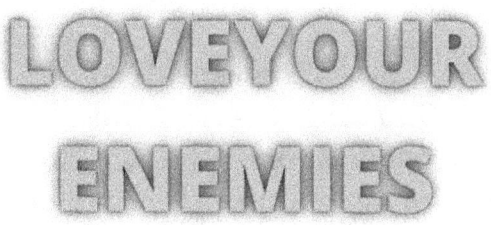

Devotion, Inspiration & the God's Word

LOVE YOUR ENEMIES

Exodus 14:14

The Lord shall fight for you, and ye shall hold your peace.
Matthew 5:44
But I say unto you, Love your enemies, bless them that curse you, do good to them that hate you, and pray for them which despitefully use you, and persecute you;
Romans 12:14
Bless them which persecute you: bless, and curse not.

There is no need to fight your enemies, the Lord will fight All of your battles on your behalf. Pray for your enemies and open your heart to your enemies. I know it is a lot harder than it may seem but as a servant of God we must think Christ like. The power that is behind loving your enemies is beyond what you may see on the surface. The root to love is the power of redemption.

****

Prayer:
**Oh Father God in Heaven,
I stand before you and ask for guidance and strength to love those that persecute me, to love those that hate me, to love those that come against me. Help me lord to continue to fight their evil ways with peace and good. At times I get weary and want to fight evil for evil. I trust in your word that you will fight for me! I will continue to trust in your hedge of protection and hold my peace. In Jesus Name I pray!
Amen!**

FORGIVENESS

Devotion, Inspiration & the God's Word

FORGIVENESS

1 John 1:9

If we confess our sins, he is faithful and just to forgive us our sins, and to cleanse us from all unrighteousness.

Mark 11:25

And when ye stand praying, forgive, if ye have ought against any: that your Father also which is in heaven may forgive you your trespasses.

Colossians 3:13

Forbearing one another, and forgiving one another, if any man have a quarrel against any even as Christ forgave you, so also do ye.

Forgiveness is for you! Forgiveness free you from bondage and allows you to move on without seeking revenge or holding on to anymore contempt, anger, or hurt. Just as you want the Father to forgive you for your sins, you must forgive others for their sins against you.

We are not perfect, but we strive for perfection. There are going to be times where mistakes will be made. It does not make sense to continue to hold onto those

mistakes in carry that negative energy around! Forgive and Release your Trespasses and live Freely through Christ our father in Heaven!

****

Prayer:
Oh Father God in Heaven,
Please place in me a heart of forgiveness. I no longer want to hold onto the past. I am ready to release this anger, hurt, and disappointment. Just as you have forgiven me for my sins, I ask that you place it in my heart to forgive all who have negatively impacted my life. I am ready to be free from this bondage placed over my life. I trust in your word and truth Lord. On this day forward, I will forgive and Release it all to you! In Jesus Name I pray!
Amen!

Devotion, Inspiration & the God's Word

FASTING

Matthew 4:2

And when he had fasted forty days and forty nights, he was afterward an hungered.
Matthew 6:16-18
Moreover when ye fast, be not, as the hypocrites, of a sad countenance: for they disfigure their faces, that they may appear unto men to fast. Verily I say unto you, They have their reward. But thou, when thou fastest, anoint thine head, and wash thy face; That thou appear not unto men to fast, but unto thy Father which is in secret: and thy Father, which seeth in secret, shall reward thee openly.
Psalm 69:10
When I wept, and chastened my soul with fasting, that was to my reproach.
Psalm 35:13
But as for me, when they were sick, my clothing was sackcloth: I humbled my soul with fasting; and my prayer returned into mine own bosom.

Jesus fasted for forty days without

eating and Satan tempted him three times. Fasting builds your spiritual growth and strengthens your faith. It is very important to participate in fasting as a servant of God.

Fasting allows you to bow down to God and account for your need for him in all areas of your life. You are making a sacrifice to the Lord. You are rejecting your physical body to strengthen your spiritual connection with the Most High God. It is a way to deny yourself and humble yourself before God. Fasting builds focus, awareness, discipline, and reminds us of our dependent on God.

****

Prayer:
Oh Father God in Heaven,
I come before you as your humble servant. I ask that you continue to strengthen me spiritually, mentally, emotionally, and physically. I am submitting to your purpose and will. I am dying daily from my sins through the renewal of your spirit within me. Continue to lead me and deliver me from evil and help me to take refuge in your open arms. With every

temptation formed against me I pray for your guidance to escape and conquer it.
In Jesus Name I pray!
Amen!

Devotion, Inspiration & the God's Word

Devotion, Inspiration & the God's Word

PRAYER

Psalms 55:17

Evening, and morning, and at noon, will I pray, and cry aloud: and he shall hear my voice.

John 14:13-14

And whatsoever ye shall ask in my name, that will I do, that the Father may be glorified in the Son. If ye shall ask any thing in my name, I will do it.

Philippians 4:6

Be careful for nothing; but in every thing by prayer and supplication with thanksgiving let your requests be made known unto God.

Luke 11:9

And I say unto, Ask, and it shall be given you; seek, and ye shall find; knock, and it shall be opened unto you.

1 Thessalonians 5:17

Pray without ceasing.

Devotion, Inspiration & the God's Word

Prayer is a form of communication between us and God. Crying aloud to our Father in prayer three times a day is necessary. When we awake, noonday, and before bed. Prayer can be used to ask for help, or forgiveness. Prayer can be spoken out loud, silent with no talking, or in a song through worship. Prayer is an act of worship to reinforce our need for God. We shouldn't refrain anything from prayer and never stop praying.

You may use prayer to pray on your behalf as well as others. God hears our prayers and our requests are being known.

We should pray over situations; we should pray before we make decisions. Do not be hasty in judgement and when we pray follow the signs of God. Nothing is off limits when speaking to the Father. For he already knows our hearts and will guide us accordingly to his will and your purpose. Continue to pray and trust in the results of your prayer.

Believe in your prayers and never stop Praying!

****

Prayer:
Oh Father God in Heaven,
How bless are we to have prayer, how blessed are we to be able to talk directly to you. I am so thankful for my blessings in advanced. I am so thankful for you always being by my side. I make my request to you over my life and you align my path based off my purpose. I am so thankful Father! In Jesus Name I pray!
Amen!

Devotion, Inspiration & the God's Word

SPIRITUAL WAREFARE

Ephesians 6:12-13

For we wrestle not against flesh and blood, but against principalities, against powers, against the rulers of the darkness of this world, against spiritual wickedness in high places. Wherefore take unto you the whole armor of God, that ye may be able to withstand in the evil day, having done all, to stand.

Romans 8:6-7

For to be carnally minded is death; but to be spiritually minded is life and peace. Because the carnal mind is enmity against God: for it is not subject to the law of God, neither indeed can be.

James 4:7

Submit yourselves therefore to God. Resist the devil, and he will flee for you.

We are on a daily unseen internal battle with good versus evil. It is important to repent and die daily within the spirit. For we will continue to be tempted while being visitors on this proven ground.

If you aren't spiritually guarded, you will fall weak in the battle every time. You must rebuke the devil daily and take a stance by staying obedient to the commandments of God. You will become harder to tempt if you are steadfast in his word through reading, praying, fasting, and keeping his word!

****

Prayer:
Oh Father God in Heaven,
Plead my cause oh Lord, take hold of shield and buckler and stand up for me in this daily fight with evil. I rebuke Satan and his followers! Let them be confounded and put to shame! All those that seek after me and try to attack my soul, I cast them out. Break all spells cast over my life Lord! I am your servant oh Lord and I need your continuous protection over my life! I trust in your word! In Jesus Name I pray!
Amen!

Devotion, Inspiration & the God's Word

WISDOM & KNOWLEDGE

James 1:5

If any of you lack wisdom, let him ask of God, that giveth to all men liberally, and upbraideth not; and it shall be given him.

2 Timothy 2:15

Study to shew thyself approved unto God, a workman that needeth not to be ashamed, rightly diving the word of truth.

Psalms 111:10

The fear of the Lord is the beginning of wisdom: a good understanding have all they that do his commandments: his praise endureth for ever.

We are blessed with wisdom and knowledge through obedience of keeping God's laws and commandments.

Through reading and meditating the Bible. Prayer, fasting, reading, and applying contributes to gaining wisdom and knowledge. It also increases your faith in God with having the spiritual

Devotion, Inspiration & the God's Word

knowledge to overcome the temptations of the devil. You are building your spirit up by reflecting on biblical insights daily and crying aloud in prayer.

****

Prayer:
Oh Father God in Heaven,
I come to you as your humble servant and ask for wisdom and knowledge. I sometimes get confused and don't understand what I read or how to seek you. I pray for that spirit to be delivered and released. Please help me Lord! Help me to have understanding. I pray that you strengthen my spirit with your understandings and beliefs! I ask for wisdom and knowledge in your word and through your teachings of Father God. In Jesus Name I pray!
Amen!

Devotion, Inspiration & the God's Word

DISCERNMENT

1 John 4:1

Beloved, believe not every spirit, but try the spirits whether they are of God: because many false prophets are gone out into the world.

John 7:24

Judge not according to the appearance, but judge righteous judgement.

1 Thessalonians 5:21

Prove all things; hold fast that which is good.

Matthew 10:16

Behold, I send you forth as sheep in the midst of wolves: be ye therefore wise as serpents, and harmless as doves.

Romans 12:2

And be not conformed to this world: but be ye transformed by the renewing of your mind, that ye may prove what is that good, and acceptable, and perfect, will of God.

Discernment is spiritual guidance and judgement received from God. It is being able to judge accordingly through the spirit. Spirit of discernment deals with allowing God to be your guide into

making the best decision over your life and others. It also refers to being able to spiritually understand and comprehend situations and people.

This is a blessing received from God when uprooted in his teachings and following his commandments and laws. The spirit of discernment will be upon you to see things through the spirit and not the surface. With God's word and guidance, you will have a better understanding through the spirit of God.

****

Prayer:

Oh Father God in Heaven,
I ask for forgiveness for not interpreting through your Spirit. I pray for spirit of discernment. I ask that you be my guide over my life and others. I pray for my discernment to strengthen where I can prevent unforeseen negative situations to coming to past. Help me to be a blessing to others. Help me to be a positive impact and make better decisions. I am tired of leaning on my own understanding and I ask for your spirit of discernment! I lean on you Lord and you only! Lord continue to lead me and guide me! In Jesus Name I

pray!
Amen!

Devotion, Inspiration & the God's Word

Devotion, Inspiration & the God's Word

MARRIAGE

Hebrews 13:4

Marriage honourable in all, and the bed undefiled: but whoremongers and adulterers God will judge.

Ephesians 5:22-25

Wives, submit yourselves unto your own husbands, as unto the Lord. For the husband is the head of the wife, even as Christ is the head of the church: and he is the savior of the body. Therefore as the church is subject unto Christ, so let the wives be to their own husbands in everything. Husbands, love your wives, even as Christ also loved the church, and gave himself for it;

1 Corinthians 7:4

The wife hath no power of her own body, but the husband: and likewise also the husband hath not power of his own body, but the wife.

Marriage is a beautiful blessing from God. Marriage is a divine institution between Husband and Wife which bounds them together before God to become one. God created woman to add value to the

man and serve as his helpmate.

The Husband must love their wife as he loves himself and the same for the wife. Therefore, they both must submit to each other while keeping God present in their marriage. Two is better than one. Marriage is another form of God's love for you. Through marriage and family you are able to build the nation.

****

Prayer:
Oh Father God in Heaven,
I pray over my marriage and ask for you to restore it in the areas where we fall short. I pray that me and my spouse continue to seek you within our marriage. I pray that we continue to grow in your word. I pray that our love for each other strengthen and lives on for eternity. I thank you for my spouse and I ask you to forgive all of the times where I fell short in my marriage. I ask that you continue to strengthen our communication and supply our needs. I ask for your covering and protection over our marriage. In Jesus Name I pray!
Amen!

Devotion, Inspiration & the God's Word

DIVORCE

Deuteronomy 24:1

When a man hath taken a wife, and married her, and it come to pass that she find no favour in his eyes, because he hath found some uncleanness in her: then let him write her a bill of divorcement, and give it in her hand, and send her out of his house.

Matthew 19:9

And I say unto you, Whosoever shall put away his wife, except it be for fornication, and shall marry another, committeth adultery; and whoso marrieth her which is put away doth commit adultery.

1 Corinthians 7:15

But if the unbelieving depart, let him depart. A brother or a sister is not under bondage in such cases: but God hath called to peace.

Romans 7:2

For the woman which hath an husband is bound by the law to her husband so long as he liveth; but if the husband be dead, she is loosed from the law of her husband.

Marriage was not intended for divorce. God hates divorce and intends for everlasting love between Man and Woman through marriage.

God does acknowledge divorcing in the scriptures. Sexual activity outside of the marital covenant breaks the marriage vow and covenant.

Also, if you are married to a non-believer you are not subjected to staying married to that person. In this broken world that we live in divorce is subjected to happening and the Lord was aware of this. Let's try our hardest to not go against what God has joined together.

****

Prayer:
Oh Father God in Heaven,
I know you hate divorce and hate how it tears down families and break the covenant. I ask for forgiveness and your wisdom. I need your wisdom and clarity moving forward to make God-honoring decisions. In Jesus Name I pray!
Amen!

RAISING YOUR CHILDREN

Devotion, Inspiration & the God's Word

RAISING YOUR CHILDREN

Proverbs 22:6

Train up a child in the way he should go: and when he is old, he will not depart from it.

Proverbs 23:13

Withhold not correction from the child: for if thou beatest him with the rod, he shall not die.

Proverbs 29:15

The rod and reproof give wisdom: but a child left to himself bringeth his mother to shame.

Psalm 127:3

Lo, children are an heritage of the Lord: and the fruit of the womb is his reward.

Training up your children is very important and mentioned throughout the Bible. It is important to install the teachings of the Bible and be great examples to your children. Teaching your children how to pray, read their Bibles daily, and love God through keeping his commandments/laws.

Your children follow from your lead. It is also important to discipline your children and do not fall short from it. This is how respect is gained and they develop good habits, make the right decisions, and follow God into their adulthood.

****

Prayer:
Oh Father God in Heaven,
I ask that you continue to help me be a good example of your word. I pray that I am a great example to my children. Oh Lord help guide me to teach them to make righteous decision. Watch over my children where I am not present. Guide my children thoughts and ways. I ask that you continue to watch over them all the days of their lives. In Jesus Name I pray!
Amen!

Devotion, Inspiration & the God's Word

DEPRESSION ANXIETY

1 Peter 5:7

Casting all you care upon him; for he careth for you.

Isaiah 41:10, 13

Fear thou not; for I am with thee: be not dismayed; for I am thy God: I will strengthen thee; yea, I will help thee; yea, I will uphold thee with the right hand of my righteousness--- For I the Lord thy God will hold thy right hand, saying unto thee, Fear not; I will help thee.

1 Corinthians 10:13

There hath no temptation taken you but such as is common to man: but God is faithful, who will not suffer you to be tempted above that ye are able; but will with the temptation also make a way to escape, that ye may be able to bear it.

Proverbs 12:25

Heaviness in the heart of man maketh it stoop: but a good word maketh it glad.

Devotion, Inspiration & the God's Word

Depression and Anxiety does not come from the Lord. It comes from a spirit of fear and denial. Although, it is quite common for us all to experience forms of depression and anxiety living on this proving ground.

It is best for us to try to overcome this spiritual weakness through turning to the Lord. When that spirit does come over us, we must turn to the scriptures, prayers and understand that everything we are experiencing right now in life is temporary. Because Nothing last forever, but we cannot give up! This fight was not intended to be easy.

The Lord is always with us through these dark moments and times even when we cannot feel him or see him.

God is faithful over our lives, but we must first believe and strengthen our spiritual believes.

****

Prayer:
Oh Father God in Heaven,
I feel broken, I feel weak, my soul is under the pits. I need you more than ever Lord. I cant feel you near but I know through

*your word that you are near. Please heal your servant from this feeling of fear. I am tired Lord of being in this dark place within my life. I need your light to shine over my life more than ever right now Lord. I need you now Lord! Please rescue me! Please release this feeling of anxiety and depression Lord! I no longer will accept this fear over my life! I surrender it all over to you lord because this isn't my fight anymore and you shall fight for me! I trust your healing over my life. I trust you to restore my happiness and peace of mind Lord. I trust you and I thank you for healing me! In Jesus Name I pray!
Amen!*

Devotion, Inspiration & the God's Word

Devotion, Inspiration & the God's Word

HOLY SPIRIT

1 Corinthians 3:16
Know ye not that ye are the temple of God, and *that* the Spirit of God dwelleth in you?

John 14:16-18
And I will pray the Father, and he shall give you another Comforter, that he may abide with you for ever; Even the spirit of truth; whom the world cannot receive, because it seeth him not, neither knoweth him: but ye know him; for he dwelleth with you, and shall be in you. I will not leave you comfortless: I will come to you.

John 14:26
But the Comforter, which is the Holy Ghost, whom the Father will send in my name, he shall teach you all things, and bring all things to your remembrance, whatsoever I have said unto you.

Acts 7:55
But he, being full of the Holy Ghost, looked up stedfastly into heaven, and saw the glory of God, and Jesus standing on the right hand of God,

The Holy Spirit is our Comforter that abides within us through the word of God. Each one of us are blessed with spiritual guides aka Holy spirit within us. A blessing received from Christ that the father has sent to us in his name to lead us and bring us remembrance of his love for us, mercy, and grace!

****

Prayer:
Oh Father God in Heaven,
I am so thankful for my Holy Spirit that abides within me. There are times when I don't know which direction to turn or what to do and my Holy Spirit has guided me. Oh Lord, I ask that you continue to strengthen my Holy Spirit! Continue to allow me to become one with my spirit and hear my spirit clearer each day. In Jesus Name I pray!
Amen!

Devotion, Inspiration & the God's Word

BORN AGAIN

John 3:3

Jesus answered and said unto him, Verily, verily, I say unto thee, Except a man be born again, he cannot see the kingdom of God.

John 3:36

He that believeth on the Son hath everlasting life: and he that believeth not the Son shall not see life; but the wrath of God abideth on him.

2 Corinthians 5:17

Therefore if any man be in Christ, he is a new creature: old things are passed away; behold, all things are become new.

2 Corinthians 13:5

Examine yourselves, whether ye be in the faith, prove your own selves, Know ye not your own selves, how that Jesus Christ is in you, except y be reprobates?

1 Peter 1:23

Being born again, not of corruptible seed, but of incorruptible, by the word of God, which liveth and abideth for ever.

****

The deliverance of death and separation from God by Jesus Christ's death and resurrection allows us to be born again. To be born again means to be saved through the confession of accepting Jesus Christ as your savior and keeping God's commandments/laws. It also means to repent from your sins and turn away from them. The renewal of your mind is paramount with becoming a new creature in Christ to purge out your old ways of thinking.

****

Prayer:
Oh Father God in Heaven,
I need you, I thank you for your son Lord Jesus dying on the cross for my sins. I open my heart to you, I open the door of my life over to you to receive Jesus as my Lord and Savior. Lord I confess my sins to you. I thank you for forgiving my sins. I shall turn away from the old life and I now surrender and commit my life to you Lord from this day moving forward! In Jesus Name I pray!
Amen!

DEE EVANS

Devotion, Inspiration & the God's Word

MORE BOOKS & JOURNALS FROM DEE

"God's Voice for Prayers: 45 Psalms & Prayers"

"Rise up in Faith: Forgiveness & Repentance"

"30-Day Devotional & Inspiration for the Single Mom"

"Thoughts from a Black Woman"

"Lust, Pain & Love: A Poetry Collection"

"90-Day Gratitude Journal 4 Men"

"Her Price is far above Rubies: 90-day Self-Reflection Journal"

ABOUT THE AUTHOR

Dee Evans is a servant of the Most High, wife, and Mother. She is on a mission to write books to inspire, motivate, and uplift your spirit.

Dee is also a Book Publisher, Poet, 2xPodcaster, Life Coach, and Non-profit Consultant.

Check out Dee's Podcasts Streaming on Youtube & all major streaming sites:

"Dee Poetry & Inspiration Podcast" and "Black Girls in Faith Podcast"

Follow on Instagram, Facebook & Threads:

Authordevans

Please like me on Facebook

https://www.facebook.com/authordeeevans/

If interested in talking with Dee please visit:

https://linktr.ee/authordevans

If interested in sharing your story with the world through publishing please visit:

www.rise2write.com

www.ingramcontent.com/pod-product-compliance
Lightning Source LLC
Chambersburg PA
CBHW071906070526
44583CB00016B/1873